This book belongs to

Age

Favourite player

Prediction of Norwich City's final position this season

Prediction of Championship winners this season

Prediction of FA Cup winners this season

Prediction of League Cup winners this season

Written by twocan

Contributors: James Hyde,
Rob Mason, Peter Rogers.

A TWOCAN PUBLICATION

©2016. Published by twocan under
licence from Norwich City FC.

ISBN 978-1-909872-98-1

PICTURE CREDITS
Action Images, Jasonpix, Press Association.

06	Goals, Goals, Goals		37	Jonny Howson Poster
08	The Squad 2016-17		38	Who are Yer?
18	Timm Klose Poster		40	Canaries at the Euros
19	Spot the Season		42	Alex Tettey Poster
20	Skills: The Cruyff Turn		43	Spot the Season
21	Cult Heroes: Darren Eadie		44	A-Z of the Championship - Part 2
22	Football and Fitness		46	Design your own Footie Boots
24	Player of the Season		47	Robbie Brady Poster
25	Goal of the Season		48	Fan'tastic
26	A-Z of the Championship - Part 1		50	Cameron Jerome Poster
28	Dream Team		51	Cult Heroes: Darren Huckerby
30	Wes Hoolahan Poster		52	Skills: The Maradona Spin
31	On the Road		53	Club or Country?
32	Championship Danger Men		54	Josh Murphy Poster
36	Skills: The Rainbow Kick		55	Hat-trick Heroes

Contents

56	Wonderkid
57	Spot the Season
58	Cult Heroes: Robert Fleck
59	Ivo Pinto Poster
60	2016-17 Predictions
62	Quiz Answers

GOALS, GOALS Goals

STEVEN NAISMITH
V BLACKBURN ROVERS

CAMERON JEROME
V BLACKBURN ROVERS

CAMERON JEROME
V IPSWICH TOWN

JONNY HOWSON V BRISTOL CITY

SERGI CANOS V COVENTRY CITY

RUSSELL MARTIN V COVENTRY CITY

JACOB MURPHY V BLACKBURN ROVERS

BEN GODFREY V COVENTRY CITY

THE SQUAD 2016-17

Steven WHITTAKER | 02

POSITION: Defender   **NATIONALITY:** Scottish   **DOB:** 16.06.1984

DID YOU KNOW? Despite beginning his career at Hibernian, Whittaker was a childhood fan of Hibs' rivals Hearts.

John RUDDY | 01

POSITION: Goalkeeper   **NATIONALITY:** English   **DOB:** 24.10.1986

DID YOU KNOW? Ruddy was selected for the England EURO 2012 squad, but missed the tournament due to a broken finger.

Martin OLSSON | 03

POSITION: Defender   **NATIONALITY:** Swedish   **DOB:** 17.05.1988

DID YOU KNOW? Olsson's brother-in-law is German basketball player Dirk Nowitzki who plays for the Dallas Mavericks.

Russell MARTIN | 05

POSITION: Defender   NATIONALITY: Scottish   DOB: 04.01.1986

DID YOU KNOW? Martin has spent at least two seasons in all four English Football League divisions.

Graham DORRANS | 04

POSITION: Midfielder   NATIONALITY: Scottish   DOB: 05.05.1987

DID YOU KNOW? Dorrans was named in the Championship Team of the Year for the 2009-10 season.

Sebastien BASSONG | 06

POSITION: Defender   NATIONALITY: Cameroonian   DOB: 09.07.1986

DID YOU KNOW? Bassong achieved a double promotion in 2014-15, as both Norwich and Watford (with whom he spent a loan spell) were promoted to the Premier League.

THE Squad 2016-17

Steven NAISMITH | 07

POSITION: Attacker   NATIONALITY: Scottish   DOB: 14.09.1986

DID YOU KNOW? Scottish International Steven Naismith is an ambassador for Dyslexia Scotland.

Jonny HOWSON | 08

POSITION: Midfielder   NATIONALITY: English   DOB: 21.05.1988

DID YOU KNOW? Howson first captained Leeds United at the tender age of just 19-years-old.

Nelson OLIVEIRA | 09

POSITION: Striker **NATIONALITY:** Portuguese **DOB:** 08.08.1991

DID YOU KNOW? Nelson joined from Portuguese side Benfica in the summer, having spent 2015-16 with Nottingham Forest.

Cameron JEROME | 10

POSITION: Attacker **NATIONALITY:** English **DOB:** 14.08.1986

DID YOU KNOW? Jerome, who began his career as a trainee with Huddersfield Town, has 10 England Under-21 caps.

Matt JARVIS | 11

POSITION: Midfielder **NATIONALITY:** English **DOB:** 22.05.1986

DID YOU KNOW? Both Jarvis' mother and father were England number ones in table tennis.

Robbie BRADY | 12

POSITION: Midfielder **NATIONALITY:** Irish **DOB:** 14.01.1992

DID YOU KNOW? Brady began his career at Manchester United, but made just one appearance for the Red Devils.

Paul JONES | 13

POSITION: Goalkeeper   NATIONALITY: English   DOB: 28.06.1986

DID YOU KNOW? Jones was the first goalkeeper to save a penalty at the new Wembley Stadium.

Wes HOOLAHAN | 14

POSITION: Midfielder   NATIONALITY: Irish   DOB: 20.05.1982

DID YOU KNOW? Hoolahan was selected for the Football Manager Team of the Decade in 2015.

Timm KLOSE | 15

POSITION: Defender   NATIONALITY: Swiss   DOB: 09.05.1988

DID YOU KNOW? Klose represented Switzerland at the 2012 Olympic Games in London.

THE SQUAD 2016-17

Youssouf MULUMBU | 18

POSITION: Midfielder   NATIONALITY: Congolese   DOB: 25.01.1987

DID YOU KNOW? Born in Kinshasa, Zaire, now DR Congo, Mulumbu's first professional club was Paris St Germain.

Sergi CANOS | 17

POSITION: Midfielder   NATIONALITY: Spanish   DOB: 02.02.1997

DID YOU KNOW? Canos scored Brentford Town's Goal of the Season in the 2015-16 campaign.

Kyle LAFFERTY | 19

POSITION: Attacker   NATIONALITY: Northern Irish   DOB: 16.09.1987

DID YOU KNOW? Lafferty is Northern Ireland's second-highest goal-scorer of all time, behind former Canary David Healy.

THE Squad 2016-17

Alex PRITCHARD | 21

POSITION: Midfielder **NATIONALITY:** English **DOB:** 03.05.1993

DID YOU KNOW? Pritchard began his youth career at West Ham United and has represented England at U20 & U21 level.

Jacob MURPHY | 22

POSITION: Attacker **NATIONALITY:** English **DOB:** 24.02.1995

DID YOU KNOW? Murphy won League One Player of the Month for November 2015 while on loan to Coventry City.

Ivo
PINTO |25

POSITION: Defender   NATIONALITY: Portuguese   DOB: 07.01.1990

DID YOU KNOW? Pinto was selected for the full Portuguese squad in 2014, but did not make an appearance.

Ryan
BENNETT |24

POSITION: Defender   NATIONALITY: English   DOB: 06.03.1990

DID YOU KNOW? Bennett is a keen guitarist and has often performed at open mic nights in Norwich city centre.

Michael
TURNER |26

POSITION: Defender   NATIONALITY: English   DOB: 09.11.1983

DID YOU KNOW? Turner took part in an apprenticeship with Italian giants Internazionale in his late teens.

THE Squad 2016-17

Alexander TETTEY | 27

POSITION: Midfielder   NATIONALITY: Norwegian   DOB: 04.04.1986

DID YOU KNOW? Although Tettey was born in Accra, Ghana, he is a full Norwegian international.

Carlton MORRIS | 30

POSITION: Attacker   NATIONALITY: English   DOB: 16.12.1995

DID YOU KNOW? All of Morris' senior goals have come in Scotland while on loan to Hamilton Academical.

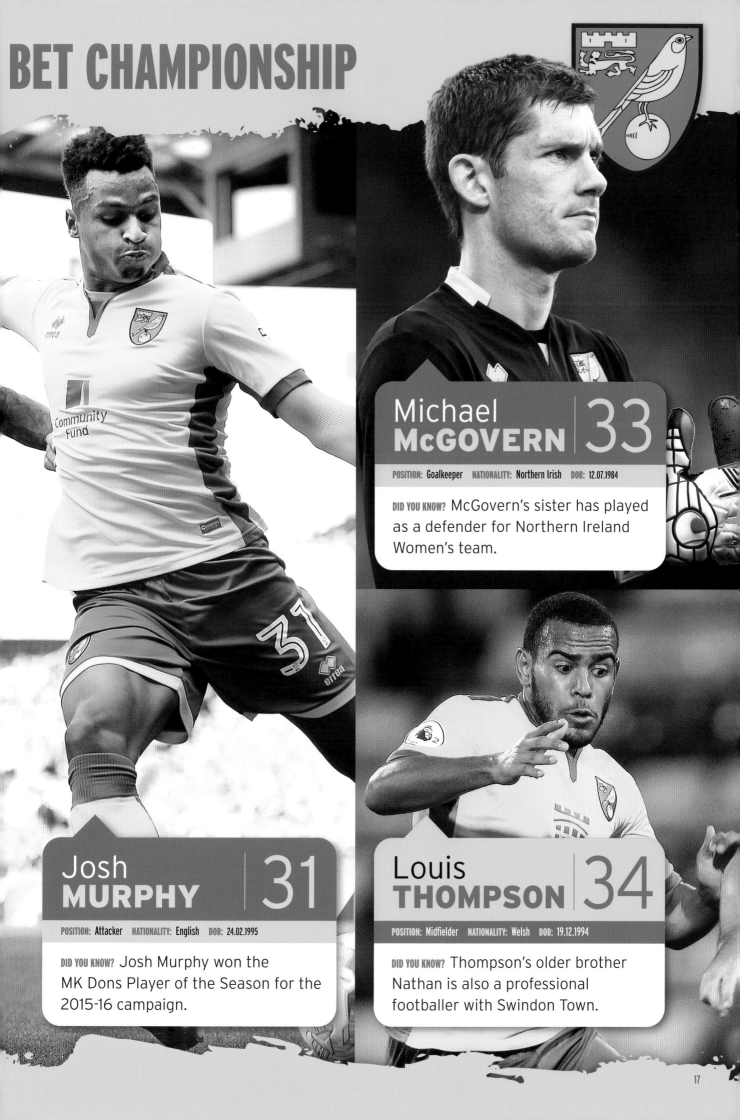

Michael McGOVERN | 33

POSITION: Goalkeeper   NATIONALITY: Northern Irish   DOB: 12.07.1984

DID YOU KNOW? McGovern's sister has played as a defender for Northern Ireland Women's team.

Josh MURPHY | 31

POSITION: Attacker   NATIONALITY: English   DOB: 24.02.1995

DID YOU KNOW? Josh Murphy won the MK Dons Player of the Season for the 2015-16 campaign.

Louis THOMPSON | 34

POSITION: Midfielder   NATIONALITY: Welsh   DOB: 19.12.1994

DID YOU KNOW? Thompson's older brother Nathan is also a professional footballer with Swindon Town.

TIMM
Klose

15

Can you spot the season from these five clues?

spot the Season

Manager Nigel Worthington

Keeper Robert Green was ever-present this season

City won eight of their last nine games

The Canaries were promoted to the Premier League as champions with 94 points, finishing eight points ahead of runners-up West Bromwich Albion

Top goalscorer with 14 league goals was Darren Huckerby

ANSWER ON PAGE 62

SKILLS: THE CRUYFF TURN

1 Draw back your foot as if you are going to kick the ball

2 Instead of following through, stop your foot over the ball ...

3 ...and push it back behind your other leg while starting to turn your body.

4 Finish turning through 180° and head in the opposite direction.

5 Your unsuspecting opponent will be left standing wondering what just happened!

Johan Cruyff unveiled his signature dummy at the 1974 FIFA World Cup. The trick is a brilliant manoeuvre to fool your opponent and change direction.

CULT heroes

With blistering pace and the ability to get fans up and out of their seats, flying winger Darren Eadie was a real crowd favourite at Carrow Road for a six-year spell between 1993 and 1999.

His performances are fondly remembered by the supporters who were fortunate enough to have witnessed them and not surprisingly his name sits proudly in the Club's Hall of Fame and also in the Canaries' Greatest Ever line-up.

DARREN EADIE

After progressing through the youth and reserve ranks, Eadie made a memorable senior debut for the Canaries as an 18-year-old substitute in the 3-0 UEFA Cup win over Vitesse Arnhem that marked the Club's entry into European football in September 1993.

Eadie's pace always gave the team an exciting cutting edge and real hope of something special for those watching in the stands. He was also a useful goalscorer; during the 1996-97 season he fired home 17 league goals and was voted supporters' player of the season.

A regular performer for England at U21 level, he was called into the senior squad in the summer of 1997. Frustratingly he suffered a number of long-term injuries which halted his progress at Carrow Road and in December 1999, after playing just over 200 games for City, he linked up again with former Canaries boss Martin O'Neill, who paid £3m to take him to Leicester City.

Sadly, Eadie's appearances for the Foxes were severely limited by injury, and in the summer of 2003 he was forced to retire at the age of just 28. He has since returned to Norfolk to live and is working locally with Langley School and to organise high profile fixture Jamie's Game with the Norwich City Community Sports Foundation.

DATE OF BIRTH:
10 June 1975

PLACE OF BIRTH:
Chippenham

CITY APPEARANCES:
204

CITY GOALS:
38

PLAYER OF THE SEASON:
1996-97

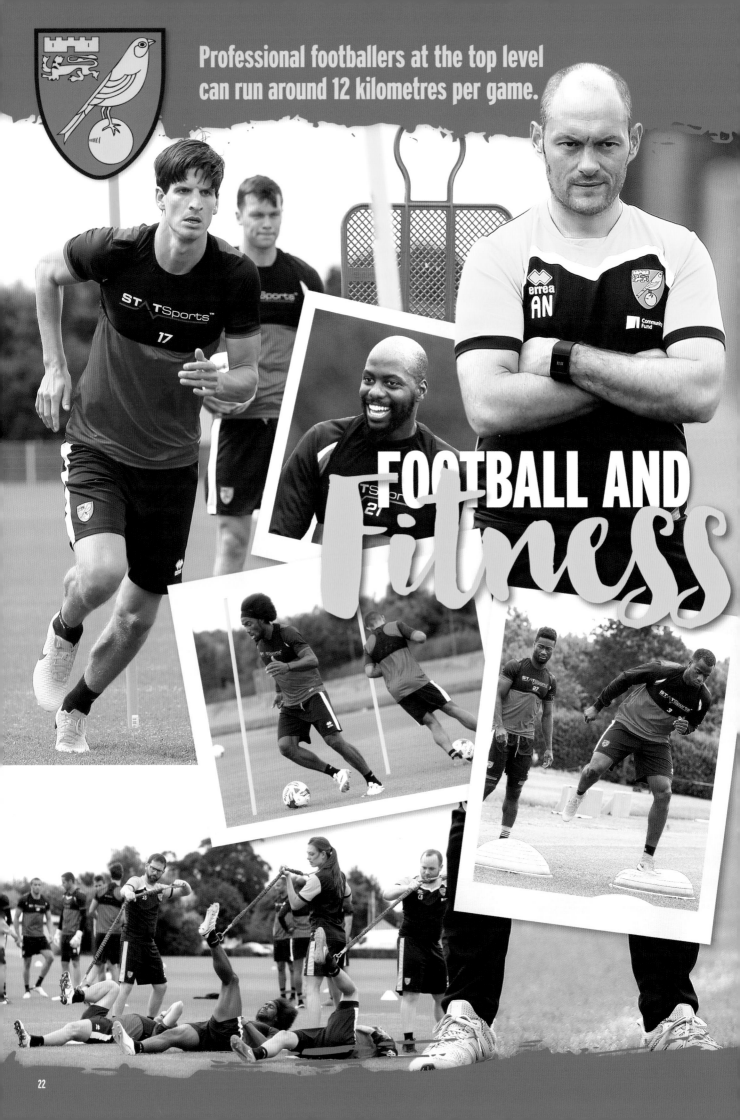

Professional footballers at the top level can run around 12 kilometres per game.

FOOTBALL AND
fitness

Quite often, they might have to play two matches within three or four days of each other and over the course of a season, regular players could play in the region of 50 games!

That would be a lot if they were simply running as a long distance runner does. In football though, that running is done with a mixture of short sprints from a standing start and runs of various lengths at differing intensities. On top of this, there is a lot of twisting and turning, often while someone is trying to pull the player back or even kick them.

If they can cope with this, there is then the consideration that once the footballer has the ball, they have to use it, either with a telling pass or a shot on goal, while the opposition do all they can to stop them.

To cope with all this, players have to be supremely fit so they have the stamina to last 90 minutes on a regular basis, and have the competitive edge to deal with opponents trying to stop them. Players also have to be careful to eat and drink the right things, get the right amount of sleep and keep themselves in tip-top shape.

In the summer when players return from a few weeks off, they do a lot of physical training to get themselves ready for the big kick-off. Once a few games have been played and they have, what players call, 'match-fitness', their aim is to maintain that fitness, but not over-do things.

Most players will train for two or three hours most days and do additional work in the gym, as well as perhaps doing pilates or yoga to help look after their bodies. Cycling and swimming can be useful too, but so is knowing when to simply rest, because the Championship season is a long and gruelling campaign.

PLAYER OF THE SEASON...

Jonny Howson won the Barry Butler Memorial Trophy for the first time in May 2016, after making 34 appearances for City in all competitions and chipping in with several vital goals as the Club narrowly failed to avoid relegation to the Championship.

Howson took home the Club's Player of the Season award after edging out strong competition from Republic of Ireland international Robbie Brady. The Yorkshireman proved a solid and reliable presence for City, performing capably on both the right and centre of midfield, as well as captaining the side in the absence of Russell Martin and Alexander Tettey.

The Morley-born 28-year-old began his career with local side Leeds United, rising the ranks to make his senior bow in 2006. He captained the Whites for much of their promotion-winning campaign of 2009-10, playing alongside future Canaries Robert Snodgrass, Bradley Johnson, and Luciano Becchio.

After being made permanent skipper of the Elland Road outfit in 2011, Howson moved to Norwich City for an undisclosed fee in January 2012. Across his time in Norfolk, Howson has netted his fair share of spectacular individual strikes, including a solo effort against Manchester City in 2013 and a rising half-volley against Stoke City in 2016, and his goal total, at the time of writing, stands at 19. Following his Player of the Year award, Howson started the 2016-17 season in fine fettle, captaining the side in their early fixtures and netting a well-placed winner against Bristol City in the Club's second home game of the campaign.

Goal of the Season

Jonny Howson also won the Goal of the Season award for his stunning half-volley from 20 yards out, that drew Norwich level with Stoke City at the Britannia Stadium in the Potteries on January 13, 2016.

Seizing upon a neat knock-down from Belgian midfielder Vadis Odjidja Ofoe, the former Leeds United midfielder drove a rising effort into the top corner, past the despairing dive of England international goalkeeper Jack Butland - a man who had produced an excellent display during the clubs' previous meeting at Carrow Road.

This - the sides' second encounter of the Premier League campaign - had begun cagily, but the dynamic changed when the Canaries' midfielder Gary O'Neil was handed a straight red card for a misjudged challenge on the Potters' Dutch playmaker Ibrahim Afellay. Stoke grabbed the initiative when former Ipswich striker Jonathan Walters headed home at the back post, but the Canaries superbly pegged their hosts back through Howson's well-struck leveller.

However, Stoke's numerical advantage eventually told when Spanish striker Joselu fizzed a low shot past Norwich stopper Declan Rudd. An unfortunate own-goal from Norwich centre-back Ryan Bennett secured victory for the Potters.

& THE GOAL...

JONNY
Howson

A Newcastle were relegated to the Championship last season after finishing 18th, but this club was bottom of the table

B The creatures present on Brentford's club crest

C Manager of Burton Albion when they were promoted from League One last season

D Preston North End play their home games here

E Wolves midfielder who was in Wales' squad for Euro 2016

F Name of Brighton's stadium before it was sponsored by AMEX

G Reading's top appearance maker last season

26

The answer to each clue begins with the corresponding letter of the alphabet.

H — Blackburn's player of the 2015-16 season

I — Derby County play their home games here

Leeds United's kit manufacturer

J — Wigan's Finnish goalie who helped them reach promotion last season

K

L — Huddersfield played their home games here before the John Smith's Stadium

M — The scorer of Birmingham's winning goal when they won the League Cup in 2011

DAVE WATSON

KEVIN KEELAN

STEVE BRUCE

Bruce scored the winner against Ipswich Town in the semi-final of the 1985 League Cup, was man of the match when winning the final, won the second division with City in 1986 and led them to fifth in the top flight.

Captain when the League Cup was won in 1985, Watson had a great partnership with Bruce. A promotion winner with Norwich in 1982, he later excelled with Everton and England.

In 17 seasons between 1963 and 1980, Keelan played more games for Norwich than anyone else has ever achieved – 673! Kevin liked to be spectacular and not just when making saves, sometimes he liked to take crosses one handed!

MARK BOWEN

One short of 400 appearances with City, but not short of anything else. Scored when Bayern Munich were beaten in Munich and part of the team that finished third in the Premier League's first season. Capped 41 times by Wales.

DREAM

MARTIN PETERS

DARREN EADIE

A product of City's youth system, Eadie was a dangerous winger whose best season saw him score 17 goals in 42 games in 1996-97, when he was named in the PFA Division One Team of the Season.

A World Cup winner with England in 1966 when he scored in the final, Peters was said to be 'ten years ahead of his time' so Norwich probably did well to sign him in 1975. He was great value, playing 232 times and scoring 50 times.

TED MacDOUGALL

A powerful centre-forward capable of mixing it with tough defenders, Supermac made his debut for Scotland while with Norwich. In 1975-76 he notched 23 goals as part of a tally of 51 in 112 games with the Canaries.

IAN CULVERHOUSE

Right-back who made 369 appearances for the Canaries and he later served as assistant manager. Player of the Year in 1991, he had won a championship medal with the Canaries in 1986.

MARTIN O'NEILL

Manager of the Republic of Ireland at Euro 2016, Martin also managed Norwich as well as playing for the Canaries. A former European Cup winner, O'Neill was a dynamic midfielder who inspired the City to promotion in 1982.

CHRIS SUTTON

Initially a centre-half, Sutton excelled as a forward playing for England and winning the Premier League with Blackburn. His best year at Carrow Road in 1993-94, saw him score 28 goals, 25 of them in the Premier League.

JOHNNY GAVIN

With 132 goals, Johnny Gavin is the Canaries all-time top scorer - even though he was a winger. He played 338 games after signing from Limerick.

29

WES **Hoolahan** 14

On the Road

Do you know where every Championship team plays their home games?

Fill in the missing words and find all the grounds in the grid!

S	R	F	C	A	R	R	O	W	R	O	A	D	S	L	N	A	L	F	S	J	D
E	A	T	O	A	K	W	E	L	L	S	T	A	D	I	U	M	U	K	V	O	F
Y	S	K	W	S	R	I	A	E	K	O	W	O	N	T	F	E	X	B	A	H	G
Q	I	F	M	V	M	D	R	S	J	G	L	D	S	A	W	X	C	T	X	N	I
W	S	K	U	I	U	L	I	B	H	E	S	N	J	O	M	S	I	S	D	S	P
N	K	G	I	L	I	E	C	F	S	T	B	H	O	U	C	T	T	M	A	M	M
A	E	R	D	L	D	M	V	Y	F	A	O	D	G	Y	L	A	Y	U	O	I	U
P	L	I	A	A	A	R	G	L	D	C	P	N	Y	E	N	D	G	I	R	T	I
O	A	F	T	P	T	U	J	R	O	A	I	S	G	D	Y	I	R	D	D	H	D
R	D	F	S	A	S	V	D	V	R	F	J	T	R	A	H	U	O	A	N	S	A
T	P	I	W	R	I	E	C	K	O	B	T	E	Y	C	T	M	U	T	A	S	T
M	E	N	D	K	K	Z	M	T	M	D	W	U	G	S	K	E	N	S	L	T	S
A	E	P	L	D	S	B	P	A	S	S	O	T	S	F	T	B	D	O	L	A	I
N	D	A	R	Q	J	F	H	N	J	I	M	Y	Z	R	U	A	O	R	E	D	L
R	C	R	A	V	E	N	C	O	T	T	A	G	E	D	O	E	D	P	N	I	L
O	U	K	E	H	D	P	V	J	F	M	S	P	C	I	P	A	R	I	G	U	E
A	E	S	S	E	A	L	N	E	W	Y	O	R	K	S	T	A	D	I	U	M	R
D	N	W	X	A	M	U	I	D	A	T	S	X	U	E	N	I	L	O	M	M	I
H	I	L	L	S	B	O	R	O	U	G	H	Q	O	H	G	S	G	E	A	T	P

Aston Villa	_ _ _ _ _ Park	**Cardiff**	_ _ _ _ _ _ _ City Stadium	**Nottm Forest**	City _ _ _ _ _ _
Barnsley	_ _ _ _ _ _ _ Stadium	**Derby**	_ _ _ _ Stadium	**Preston**	_ _ _ _ _ _ _
Birmingham	St _ _ _ _ _ _ _	**Fulham**	Craven _ _ _ _ _ _ _	**QPR**	_ _ _ _ _ _ Road
Blackburn	_ _ _ _ _ Park	**Huddersfield**	John _ _ _ _ _ _ Stadium	**Reading**	_ _ _ _ _ _ _ _ Stadium
Brentford	Griffin _ _ _ _	**Ipswich**	_ _ _ _ _ _ _ Road	**Rotherham**	AESSEAL _ _ _ _ Stadium
Brighton	_ _ _ Stadium	**Leeds**	Elland _ _ _ _	**Sheff Wed**	_ _ _ _ _ _ _ _ _ _ _
Bristol City	_ _ _ _ _ _ _ Gate	**Newcastle**	St _ _ _ _ _ Park	**Wigan**	DW _ _ _ _ _ _ _
Burton	_ _ _ _ _ _ _ Stadium	**Norwich**	_ _ _ _ _ _ Road	**Wolves**	_ _ _ _ _ _ _ _ _ Stadium

CHAMPIONSHIP DANGER MEN

ASTON VILLA
ROSS McCORMACK

One of the costliest strikers in the Championship, Scotland international McCormack cost Fulham £11m in 2014 with the Cottagers making a profit of £1m when Villa bought the Glasgow born hot-shot at the start of this season. The 30-year-old has scored over 150 goals in his career and is a man who makes many more.

BARNSLEY
TOM BRADSHAW

Having scored 20 goals in each of the last two seasons Bradshaw was disappointed to lose to Barnsley in last season's League One play-offs for Walsall - but then signed for the Tykes. Having scored a League Cup hat-trick against Championship side Forest last season, the Wales international got his first goal in this season's Championship in a South Yorkshire derby against Rotherham at the end of August.

BIRMINGHAM CITY
CLAYTON DONALDSON

Jamaican international Donaldson is a great spearhead for the Blues. Good in the air, determined and mobile he has scored over 40 goals for three different clubs and could equal that achievement with a good season for Birmingham for whom he has bagged 27 in the past two seasons.

BLACKBURN ROVERS
DANNY GRAHAM

A well-travelled target man, Danny Graham impressed on loan for Rovers last season before signing for them in the summer. With well over 100 goals in his career, Graham's best haul was 27 with Watford in 2010-11 - 24 of those were in the Championship in what was his last full season spent at this level.

BRENTFORD
SCOTT HOGAN

Hogan could be a hero for the Bees this season and be their secret weapon. Having played for six non-league clubs he was given a chance by Rochdale who he had played for at Academy level. Hogan quickly made up for lost time, a debut goal being Sky TV's 'Goal of the Day'. It was the first of 19 he got that season as he fired Rochdale to promotion, was voted Player of the Year and into the PFA League 2 team. Badly injured soon after a move to Brentford, he returned with seven goals in seven games late last season.

BRIGHTON & HOVE ALBION
TOMER HEMED

The 29-year-old Israel international is a big part of Brighton's promotion hopes. Having played in Spain as well as his home country, Hemed scored 16 goals in 40 games in his first season in English football last season and Chris Hughton will look to bring the best out of him once again this time round.

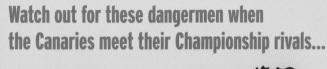

BRISTOL CITY
TAMMY ABRAHAM

With 74 goals in 98 games for Chelsea at youth level the question is can England U20 speed merchant Abraham do it at first team level? Given a Chelsea debut v Liverpool last season, he took 15 minutes of his debut on loan to Bristol City to find the net and did so four more times in his next five games. If Tammy keeps it up he could be this season's 'Rockin' Robin'.

BURTON ALBION
CHRIS O'GRADY

O'Grady has had so many loans he might think he's a high street bank, his current stint with Burton being his 10th. On loan from Brighton, Chris started this season three goals short of a century. Not always prolific, he can be - netting 15 in 2013-14 - but he's always a handful and is key to Burton doing well this season following last year's promotion.

CARDIFF CITY
RICKIE LAMBERT

Approaching 250 career goals - over 100 of them for one club (Southampton) - Rickie Lambert is a lethal finisher. The sheer number of his goals earned him an England debut in 2013 and he scored with his first touch, heading home against Scotland.

DERBY COUNTY
MATEJ VYDRA

The Rams paid a reported £8m to snap up the 24-year-old Czech Republic hitman who was the Championship Player of the Year in 2013 after netting 20 goals in 41 games for Watford. A nippy goal-poacher Vydra played in his home country as well as Italy and Belgium before coming into English football where he has also played for WBA and Reading.

FULHAM
CHRIS MARTIN

Chris Martin might feel destiny would bring him to Fulham who he joined on a season-long loan from Derby just as the transfer window closed. Having played for England at U19 level he decided to play for Scotland and made his international debut in 2014 against Nigeria ...at Fulham's Craven Cottage! Great in the air, Martin is one of the best strikers in the league.

HUDDERSFIELD TOWN
NAHKI WELLS

Having hit 17 league goals last season, Wells will hope to maintain that level of consistency for the Terriers. Nahki came to the fore at nearby Bradford City for whom he played in the League Cup final in 2013 after scoring in the semi-final against Aston Villa. Pacey, persistent and with the ability to finish, Wells is always a tough customer.

IPSWICH TOWN
BRETT PITMAN

A consistent goal-scorer who notched 11 goals for the Tractor Boys last season and 14 the year before as part of Bournemouth's title-winning team. Following Ipswich's sale of Daryl Murphy to Newcastle at the start of the season, the club's need for Pitman to be among the goals will be even more important this time round.

LEEDS UNITED
CHRIS WOOD

Twice a promotion winner to the Premier League, Leeds will hope Wood can complete a notable hat-trick at Elland Road. A New Zealand international who played at the World Cup finals in 2010, Chris won promotion to the Championship with Brighton and into the top flight with both West Brom and Leicester.

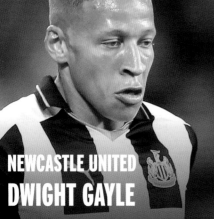

NEWCASTLE UNITED
DWIGHT GAYLE

Lift off for the man whose first club was Stansted came when Newcastle United paid £10m to bring the Londoner from Crystal Palace. Gayle's first ever Premier League goal came against Newcastle in his Palace days and he made a good start at firing the Magpies back towards the top flight with four goals in his first four games for Rafa Benitez's side.

NOTTINGHAM FOREST
BRITT ASSOMBALONGA

23 goals in 43 games for Peterborough in 2013-14 signalled Assombalonga's goal threat, Posh having already recognised that when making the Watford Academy product their record signing. A bad injury cost Britt 14 months of his career having also broken Forest's transfer record but he scored 19 goals in his first 36 games.

PRESTON NORTH END
DANIEL JOHNSON

Given a new contract early this season, Johnson is Preston's midfield creator and offers a goal threat coming in from the left. Having been schooled in the youth systems at Palace and Villa the Jamaican came to Preston in January 2015, helped North End to promotion and is at the heart of much of their best attacking play.

QUEENS PARK RANGERS
TJARONN CHERY

Hoops' Player of the Year last season, Tjaronn scored three goals in the first four games of this season, his first campaign in English football. Now 28, Chery was called into an international squad for Holland in May 2015 after scoring 15 times in his last season with Gronigen.

READING
YANN KERMORGANT

The aerial ability of the veteran French striker can be a key asset for Jaap Stam's side. Kermorgant helped Bournemouth to the Championship title in 2015 when he scored 17 goals in all competitions and was nominated for the Championship goal of the season for one of his trademark bicycle kicks.

ROTHERHAM UNITED
DANNY WARD

Rotherham will fight hard to stay up this year with Danny Ward a key man for the Millers. He scored on the opening day of the season against Wolves and soon followed that up with a vital winner against Brentford. On his day he can be lethal, as he showed with a Championship hat-trick away to Watford in May 2014 in his Huddersfield days. 25 just before Christmas, Ward's form is likely to be key to Rotherham's progress.

SHEFFIELD WEDNESDAY
STEVEN FLETCHER

Scotland international striker Fletcher spent the latter part of last season in France with Marseille - making his debut against PSG when he came on for Michy Batshuayi who Chelsea have since paid mega-money for. One of the best headers of the ball in the game, the former Hibs, Burnley, Wolves and Sunderland man can be deadly on any day of the week.

WIGAN ATHLETIC
WILL GRIGG

The song 'Will Grigg's on fire' reached the iTunes top 10 last season as the Northern Ireland international fired in 28 goals on top of the 22 he'd struck the season before. Showing no signs that his form had been dampened the 25-year-old began with a bang this term, scoring four times in his first five games. If he's heading for your defence dial 999 in case of emergency.

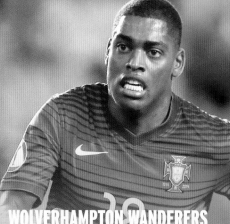

WOLVERHAMPTON WANDERERS
IVAN CAVALEIRO

As a former goalie, Wolves boss Walter Zenga knows a dangerman when he sees one and broke Wanderers' club-record to bring in Portugal international Cavaleiro for a reported £7m. The 23-year-old can play on the wing or up front and has played Champions League football for Benfica and Monaco. As an U21 international he hit a hat-trick on his debut against Switzerland in 2013.

SKILLS: THE RAINBOW KICK

1 Start off with your feet on either side of the ball

2 Use one foot to roll the ball up your other leg

3 Make sure to roll the ball hard enough to give it some air

4 When the ball is in the air strike it with your heel

5 ...and flick it over your head!

Brazilian star striker, Neymar, is well-known for his use of the rainbow kick on the pitch and regularly fools his opposition. The trick is an impressive show of skill which takes practise, practise practise!

TIP: Lean forward as you're doing the trick, this helps create space between you and the ball so you can strike it more easily.

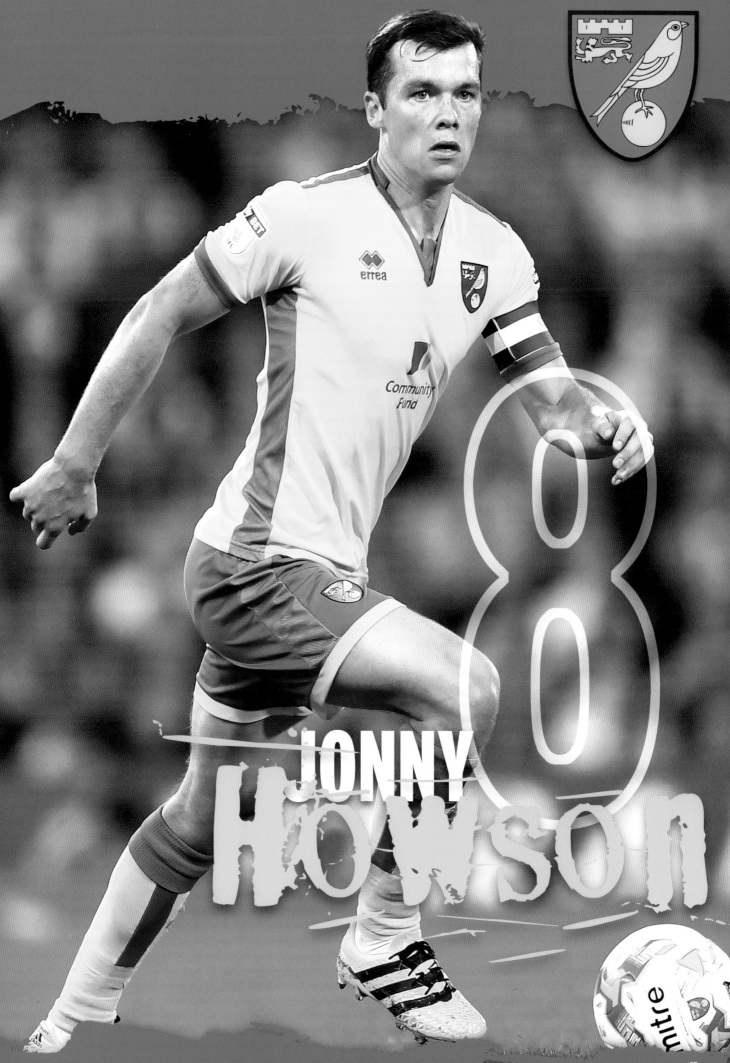

JONNY HOWSON

8

Can you identify these five Canaries?

A

B

Who

C

D

ANSWER ON PAGE 62

ARE YER

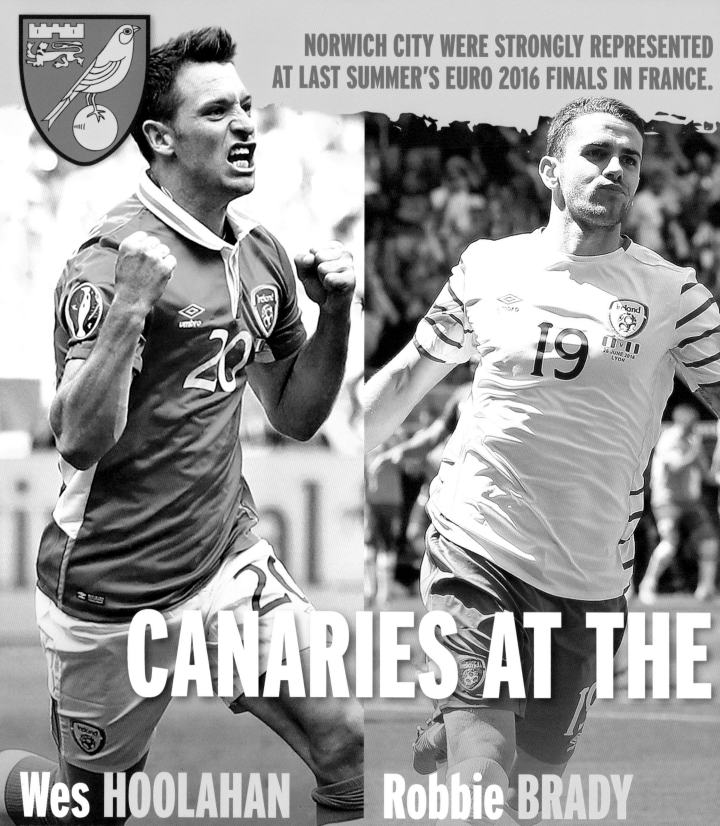

CANARIES AT THE

Wes HOOLAHAN
REPUBLIC OF IRELAND

City playmaker Wes Hoolahan took Euro 2016 by storm when he netted his country's first goal of the tournament in their opening Group E game with Sweden. Hoolahan featured in all three of the Republic's group games and set up Robbie Brady for the historic late winner against Italy that took Martin O'Neill's men through to the last 16. The Republic bowed out after a narrow defeat to hosts France, but it was an impressive showing from them and particularly Hoolahan who made a total of two starts, two substitute appearances and got his name on the scoresheet.

Robbie BRADY
REPUBLIC OF IRELAND

Undoubtedly the star performer of the five Canaries that headed to the Euros, Robbie Brady scored twice in France as his country qualified for the last 16. Brady started all four of the Republic's games and it was his memorable 85th-minute header from a Wes Hoolahan centre in Lille that took them through to the knockout stage. His hero status with the Boys in Green was enhanced even further when he calmly stepped up to convert a second-minute penalty against hosts France in the round of 16. Sadly an Antoine Griezmann brace in the second half ended the Republic's progress in the competition.

The Canary contingent chipped in with a total of 18 appearances and three goals during a memorable month of international action and all five certainly left their mark on the tournament.

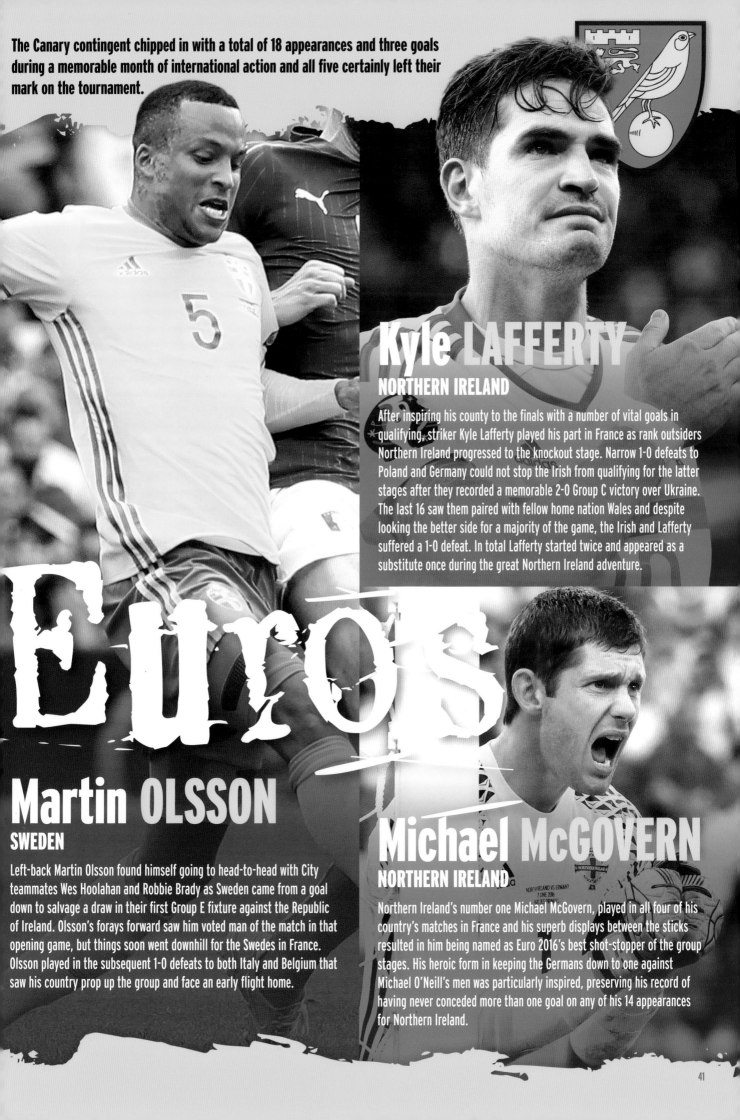

Euros

Kyle LAFFERTY
NORTHERN IRELAND

After inspiring his county to the finals with a number of vital goals in qualifying, striker Kyle Lafferty played his part in France as rank outsiders Northern Ireland progressed to the knockout stage. Narrow 1-0 defeats to Poland and Germany could not stop the Irish from qualifying for the latter stages after they recorded a memorable 2-0 Group C victory over Ukraine. The last 16 saw them paired with fellow home nation Wales and despite looking the better side for a majority of the game, the Irish and Lafferty suffered a 1-0 defeat. In total Lafferty started twice and appeared as a substitute once during the great Northern Ireland adventure.

Martin OLSSON
SWEDEN

Left-back Martin Olsson found himself going to head-to-head with City teammates Wes Hoolahan and Robbie Brady as Sweden came from a goal down to salvage a draw in their first Group E fixture against the Republic of Ireland. Olsson's forays forward saw him voted man of the match in that opening game, but things soon went downhill for the Swedes in France. Olsson played in the subsequent 1-0 defeats to both Italy and Belgium that saw his country prop up the group and face an early flight home.

Michael McGOVERN
NORTHERN IRELAND

Northern Ireland's number one Michael McGovern, played in all four of his country's matches in France and his superb displays between the sticks resulted in him being named as Euro 2016's best shot-stopper of the group stages. His heroic form in keeping the Germans down to one against Michael O'Neill's men was particularly inspired, preserving his record of having never conceded more than one goal on any of his 14 appearances for Northern Ireland.

41

ALEX Tettey 27

City reached the FA Cup semi-final as a third division side, beating Man Utd 3-0 along the way

Keeper Ken Nethercott played the last 30 minutes of the sixth round 1-1 draw at Bramall Lane with a dislocated shoulder

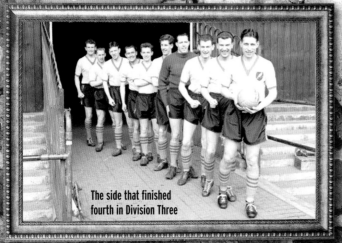

The side that finished fourth in Division Three

Archie Macaulay, the Canaries boss

Terry Bly finished top of the scoring charts with 29 in all competitions

spot the Season

Here's the second half...

N

QPR manager Jimmy Floyd Hasselbaink played for this national team

O

He scored the winning goal when Ipswich won the FA Cup in 1978

P

Fulham captain and former England international

One of Brentford's main rivals

Q

R

Aston Villa defender who has won a Premier League title with Manchester City

S

The team Norwich beat in the final of the League Cup in 1985

The answer to each clue begins with the corresponding letter of the alphabet.

T

U The animal on Bristol City's crest

Barnsley's nickname

Nottingham Forest's number 24

V

W Sheffield Wednesday's goalie

X Newcastle manager, Rafa Benitez, bought and sold this Spanish midfielder while at Liverpool

Y Young Rotherham forward

Z Danish striker who signed for Cardiff this summer

DESIGn YOUR OWN FOOtiE BOOTs

ROBBIE Brady 12

Fan 'TASTIC

There are five Great British Olympians hidden in the Canaries crowd.

Can you find them?

CULT *heroes*

DARREN HUCKERBY

Possibly one of the most exciting player to ever pull on the famous yellow Norwich shirt, Darren Huckerby produced a host of electrifying displays over a five-year Carrow Road playing career.

Although a right-footed player, Huckerby usually caused havoc in opposition defences by cutting in from his favoured position on the left wing. His pace, skill, vision, dribbling ability, powerful shooting, and unselfish willingness to set up opportunities for teammates swiftly endeared him to Canary supporters, who voted him player of the season in both 2004-05 and 2006-07.

Huckerby was a vital figure in the 2003-04 promotion campaign as he helped Nigel Worthington's squad to Premier League promotion as Nationwide First Division champions.

Initially joining the Canaries on a three-month loan deal from Manchester City in September 2003, Huckerby's impact was instant, but the Canaries and Manchester City appeared unable to thrash out a permanent deal. The player himself underlined his value in the final match of his initial loan on December 13, 2003 when he scored a stunning individual effort in the 4-1 demolition of Cardiff. The player then returned to Manchester City, but to the Canary fans' relief he was eventually unveiled as a permanent Norwich player on Boxing Day following the completion of a £750,000 deal.

A scorer of stunning goals, the most remarkable of which is generally agreed to be the strike that condemned Birmingham to a 1-0 defeat at Carrow Road in March 2007. Huckerby picked up the ball on the left-wing inside his own half, and beat four or five Birmingham players before drilling the ball home from the edge of the area.

After ending his playing days in the United States with Major League Soccer side San Jose Earthquakes, he is now a coach at the Canaries' Academy.

DATE OF BIRTH: **23 April 1976**

PLACE OF BIRTH: **Nottingham**

POSITION: **Forward**

CITY APPEARANCES: **203**

CITY GOALS: **48**

PLAYER OF THE SEASON:
2004-05 and 2006-07

51

SKILLS: THE MARADONA SPIN

1 Start off by simply dribbling the ball

2 While moving in a forward motion, tap the ball with your leading foot...

3 ...and start turning your body in the opposite direction

4

5 As you're spinning, pull the ball back with your other foot while continuing to turn

6 Then keep moving forward!

Argentinian maestro, Maradona, is very well-known for this move. It is brilliant for overcoming opponents and getting yourself into space, as while you are spinning you are putting your back to the defender and shielding the ball.

CLUB OR COUNTRY?

Can you work out which Premier League Club, Championship Club or Country each set of clues is pointing to...

1.

2.

3.

4.

5.

6.

7.

8.

9.

ANSWERS ON PAGE 62

53

31

JOSH
Murphy

SIMEON JACKSON

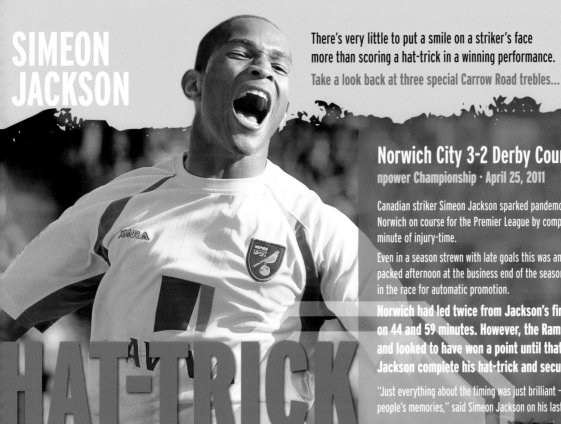

There's very little to put a smile on a striker's face more than scoring a hat-trick in a winning performance.

Take a look back at three special Carrow Road trebles...

HAT-TRICK

Norwich City 3-2 Derby County
npower Championship · April 25, 2011

Canadian striker Simeon Jackson sparked pandemonium at Carrow Road as he kept Norwich on course for the Premier League by completing a dramatic hat-trick in the sixth minute of injury-time.

Even in a season strewn with late goals this was an extraordinary finale to a tension packed afternoon at the business end of the season as the win kept City ahead of Cardiff in the race for automatic promotion.

Norwich had led twice from Jackson's first two goals of the afternoon on 44 and 59 minutes. However, the Rams came back on each occasion and looked to have won a point until that late, late winner which saw Jackson complete his hat-trick and secure a vital three points.

"Just everything about the timing was just brilliant – it's one that'll definitely live in a lot of people's memories," said Simeon Jackson on his last-gasp hat-trick against Derby County.

Norwich City 3 Southampton 1
Coca-Cola Championship Saturday, December 17, 2005

Despite struggling to make the impact most had hoped for at Championship level following relegation seven months earlier, City and Dean Ashton in particular turned on the style to record an impressive victory over Southampton.

The result proved to a be a pre-Christmas treat for the Carrow Road faithful as Ashton cancelled out the Saints' earlier opener with his first of the afternoon on 30 minutes when he headed home a Darren Huckerby cross.

The striker's second goal of the game came on 51 minutes as he powerfully headed in a Youssef Safri centre. His first hat-trick in Canary colours was complete after 66 minutes when he crashed an unstoppable volley past Saints' keeper Antti Niemi.

"I'd been through a bit of a barren spell, so it was nice to get back with a bit of a bang and the first hat-trick you get for a team is always special," recalled the City striker.

DEAN ASHTON

HEROES

Norwich City 4-1 Ipswich Town
npower Championship · November 28, 2010

Grant Holt marked his East Anglian derby debut with a thrilling lunchtime hat-trick to give 10-man Ipswich Town a painful Sunday roasting as the Canaries marched on to promotion under Paul Lambert in 2010-11.

Holt became the first Norwich player ever to score a league hat-trick against Town, and the first to net a hat-trick against the old enemy since Hugh Curran bagged three goals in a 4-2 League Cup victory at Portman Road in 1968. Holt, sporting a 'Movember' moustache, netted twice in the first half as City led 2-1 at the break and completed his hat-trick on 76 minutes.

"I think we wanted to go out and make a statement and once we went a goal up, we never really looked back," Grant Holt reflected on his successful afternoon.

GRANT HOLT

Jacob MURPHY

Born in Wembley, Jacob Murphy joined local side Queens Park Rangers at youth level alongside his twin brother Josh.

Playing in the Rangers youth team alongside current England international Raheem Sterling, the twins moved to Norwich City as Under-12s in 2006. After progressing through the youth ranks with the Canaries, both twins played vital roles in City's famous FA Youth Cup triumph of 2013. Jacob assisted brother Josh's goal in the second leg of the final, as the yellows secured a 4-2 aggregate victory over a Blues side who suffered their only loss in the competition between 2011 and 2013.

Jacob Murphy made his professional debut eight months after City's FA Youth Cup victory, coming on as a substitute for Josh in an FA Cup tie against Fulham. With City fighting against Premier League relegation, Murphy was loaned out to gain senior experience, taking in short-term spells at Swindon Town and Southend United. Despite impressing in a League Cup tie against Crawley Town for the Canaries in August 2014, Murphy began the next season on loan at Championship outfit Blackpool - scoring two goals in nine league appearances for the Tangerines and winning the club's Player of the Month award for November 2014. However, the Seasiders experienced a challenging season that eventually culminated in relegation, and Murphy returned to Carrow Road on New Year's Eve. He took in further loan spells at Scunthorpe United and Colchester United before the end of the 2014-15 campaign.

Murphy spent the entirety of the 2015-16 season on loan with Midlands side Coventry City. He enjoyed a natural chemistry with James Maddison and Newcastle United loanee Adam Armstrong, scoring 10 goals in all competitions and winning the League One Player of the Month award in November 2015.

The winger scored his first Norwich City senior goal on the first day of the 2015-16 season, opening the scoring with a long-range strike in a 4-1 away victory against Blackburn Rovers.

Wonder KID

Can you spot the season from these five clues?

Chris Woods won his first England cap while still a City player

The Gaffer, Ken Brown

Steve Bruce scored an own-goal on his debut at home to Liverpool

...but more than made amends by scoring the winning goal in the 2-1 League Cup semi-final victory over local rivals Ipswich Town

spot the season

Norwich City 1 Sunderland 0, Wembley Stadium

ANSWER ON PAGE 62

57

ROBERT FLECK

DATE OF BIRTH:
11 August 1965

PLACE OF BIRTH:
Glasgow

CITY APPEARANCES:
299

CITY GOALS:
84

PLAYER OF THE SEASON:
1991-92

Scoring vital and spectacular goals, Fleck quickly won the hearts of the City fans and was top-scorer for four successive seasons. A Scottish international - who played in the 1990 World Cup Finals in Italy - Fleck was a great entertainer who thrived on winding up opposition supporters and the more disliked he became by opposing fans, the more the Carrow Road faithful adored him.

His popularity was enhanced by a remarkable strike rate in cup competitions, but was twice a victim of cruel fate when City reached the FA Cup semi-finals in 1989 and 1992. Fleck missed the 1989 defeat by Everton following the sudden death of his father. Then, in 1992, he struggled in the 1-0 defeat to Sunderland after being rushed back from a rib injury suffered in the quarter-final replay against Southampton.

After being named Player of the Season in 1991-92, and having scored 66 goals in 181 matches, Fleck made a £2.1m move to Chelsea in August 1992. However, his spell at Stamford Bridge proved to be an unhappy one.

Martin O'Neill brought him back to Carrow Road in August 1995 and his popularity remained as he scored a further 18 goals in Canary colours. Fleck ended his career with a short spell at Reading before returning to live in Norfolk where he remains a regular and always popular visitor to Carrow Road.

Scottish striker Robert Fleck was idolised by the Carrow Road crowd during two spells with the Canaries that ended with him standing fourth in the Club's all-time goalscoring charts with 84 goals from 299 games.

Fleck began his career with Glasgow Rangers, but moved south when then City boss Dave Stringer paid a club-record £580,000 to bring him to Carrow Road in December 1987.

25

IVO Pinto

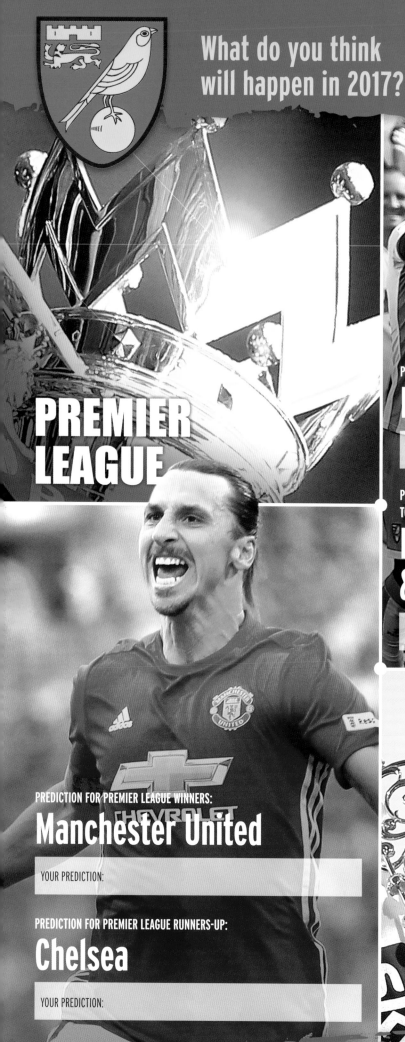

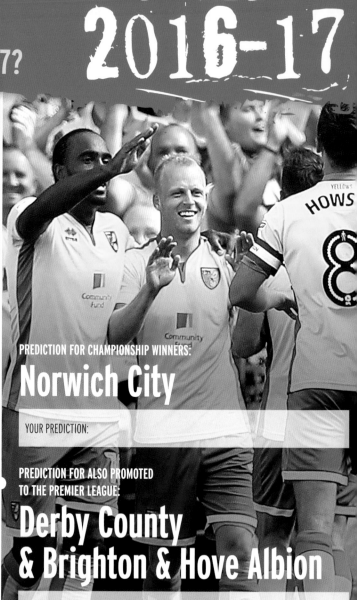

2016-17

PREMIER LEAGUE

PREDICTION FOR PREMIER LEAGUE WINNERS:

Manchester United

YOUR PREDICTION:

PREDICTION FOR PREMIER LEAGUE RUNNERS-UP:

Chelsea

YOUR PREDICTION:

PREDICTION FOR CHAMPIONSHIP WINNERS:

Norwich City

YOUR PREDICTION:

PREDICTION FOR ALSO PROMOTED
TO THE PREMIER LEAGUE:

Derby County & Brighton & Hove Albion

YOUR PREDICTION:

THE CHAMPIONSHIP

PREDICTIONS

THE FA CUP

PREDICTION FOR LEAGUE CUP WINNERS:

Arsenal

YOUR PREDICTION:

PREDICTION FOR LEAGUE CUP FINALISTS:

Everton

YOUR PREDICTION:

PREDICTION FOR FA CUP WINNERS:

Liverpool

YOUR PREDICTION:

PREDICTION FOR FA CUP FINALISTS:

Manchester City

YOUR PREDICTION:

THE LEAGUE CUP

ANSWERS

PAGE 19: SPOT THE SEASON

2003-04

PAGE 26: A-Z OF THE CHAMPIONSHIP PART 1

A. Aston Villa. B. Bees. C. Nigel Clough. D. Deepdale.
E. Dave Edwards. F. Falmer Stadium. G. Chris Gunter.
H. Grant Hanley. I. iPro Stadium. J. Jussi Jaaskelainen. K. Kappa.
I. Leeds Road. M. Obafemi Martins.

PAGE 31: ON THE ROAD

Aston Villa - Villa Park. Barnsley - Oakwell Stadium.
Birmingham - St Andrew's. Blackburn - Ewood Park.
Brentford - Griffin Park. Brighton - AMEX Stadium.
Bristol City - Ashton Gate. Burton - Pirelli Stadium.
Cardiff - Cardiff City Stadium. Derby - iPro Stadium.
Fulham - Craven Cottage. Huddersfield - John Smith's Stadium.
Ipswich - Portman Road. Leeds - Elland Road.
Newcastle - St James Park. Norwich - Carrow Road.
Nottm Forest - City Ground. Preston - Deepdale. QPR - Loftus Road.
Reading - Madejski Stadium. Rotherham - AESSEAL New York Stadium.
Sheff Wed - Hillsborough. Wigan - DW Stadium.
Wolves - Molineux Stadium.

PAGE 38: WHO ARE YER?

A. Steven Naismith. B. Robbie Brady. C. Cameron Jerome.
D. Jonny Howson. E. Ryan Bennett.

PAGE 43: SPOT THE SEASON

1958-59

PAGE 44: A-Z OF THE CHAMPIONSHIP PART 2

N. Netherlands. O. Roger Osborne. P. Scott Parker. Q. QPR.
R. Micah Richards. S. Sunderland. T. the Tykes. U. Unicorn.
V. David Vaughan. W. Keiren Westwood. X. Xabi Alonso.
Y. Jerry Yates. Z. Kenneth Zohore.

PAGE 48: FAN'TASTIC

Nicola Adams, Jessica Ennis-Hill, Andy Murray, Greg Rutherford
and Bradley Wiggins.

PAGE 53: CLUB OR COUNTRY

1. Hull City. 2. Newcastle United. 3. Spain. 4. Austria.
5. Wigan Athletic. 6. Tottenham Hotspur. 7. Iceland. 8. Arsenal.
9. Wolverhampton Wanderers.

PAGE 57: SPOT THE SEASON

1984-85